t.f.h.

all about salamanders

mervin f. roberts

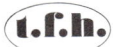

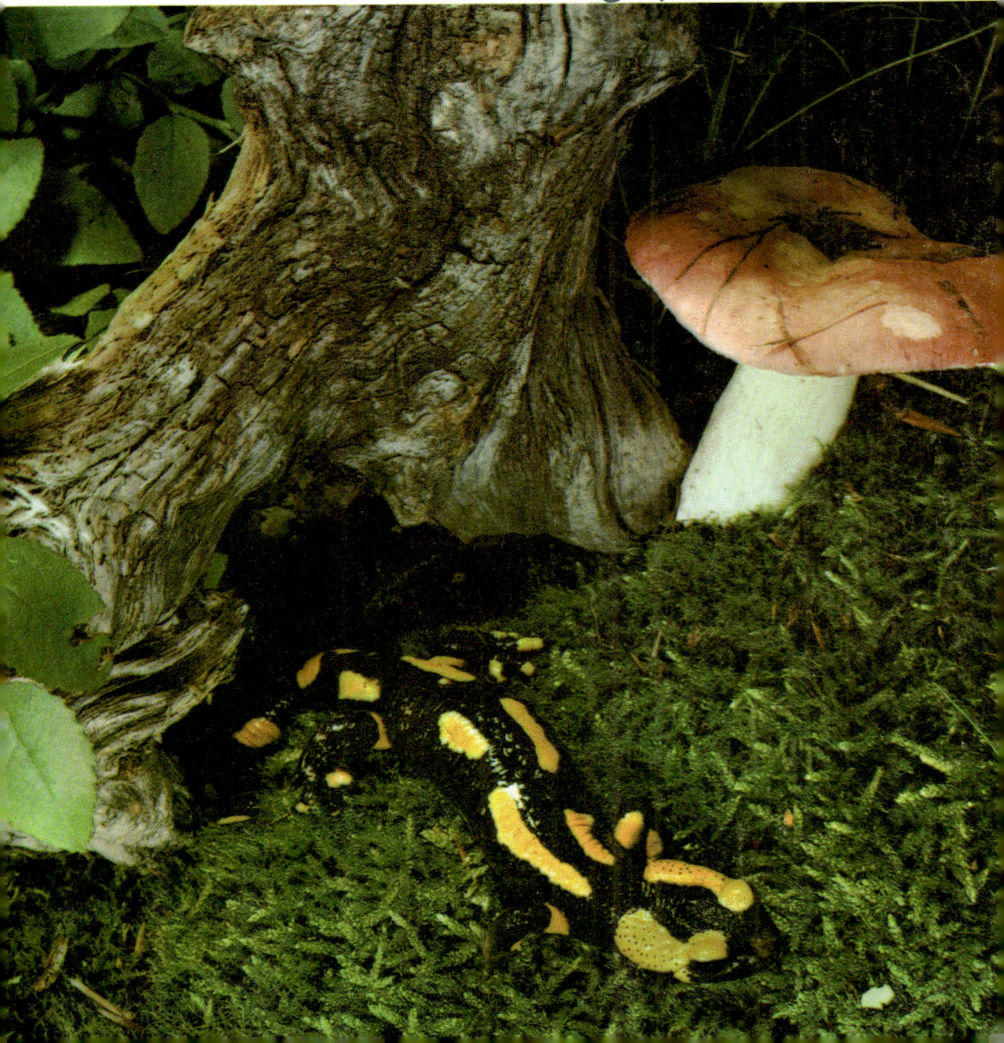

Cover:
Notophthalmus viridescens. Photo by Dr. Sherman A. Minton.

Frontispiece: European salamander, *Salamandra salamandra.* Photo by Gerhard Marcuse.

ACKNOWLEDGMENTS

The author thanks Mr. Charles D. Sullivan of Nashville, Dr. Richard G. Zweifel of New York, and Dr. Arthur English of Old Lyme, Connecticut, all of whom reviewed portions of this book and provided valuable help. John Dommers of Madison, Connecticut made many of the photographs especially for this book.

ISBN 0-87666-901-1

©1976 by T.F.H. Publications, Inc. Ltd.

Distributed in the U.S.A. by T.F.H. Publications, Inc., 211 West Sylvania Avenue, P.O. Box 27, Neptune City, N.J. 07753; in England by T.F.H. (Gt. Britain) Ltd., 13 Nutley Lane, Reigate, Surrey; in Canada to the book store and library trade by Clarke, Irwin & Company, Clarwin House, 791 St. Clair Avenue West, Toronto 10, Ontario; in Canada to the pet trade by Rolf C. Hagen Ltd., 3225 Sartelon Street, Montreal 382, Quebec; in Southeast Asia by Y.W. Ong, 9 Lorong 36 Geylang, Singapore 14; in Australia and the south Pacific by Pet Imports Pty. Ltd., P.O. Box 149, Brookvale 2100, N.S.W., Australia. Published by T.F.H. Publications, Inc. Ltd., The British Crown Colony of Hong Kong.

Contents

ACKNOWLEDGMENTS
WHAT IS A SALAMANDER? 7
CAUDATE CHARACTERISTICS 38
EXCEPTIONS 46
LONGEVITY 51
LARGER COLLECTIONS 55
REGENERATION 66
HOUSING 67
FOODS 70
RESPIRATION 73
REPRODUCTION 76
BREEDING IN CAPTIVITY 78
TRANSPORTATION 84
POPULATION DENSITY 86
TOXINS 88
DISEASES 90
SUMMING UP 94
SELECTED READING LIST 95
INDEX 96

Cryptobranchus and *Siren* are among the few salamanders that are known to feed on crayfish in their natural habitat. Apparently the exoskeleton of this crustacean is too hard for other salamanders and newts and the claws too dangerous. Photo by Dr. Herbert R. Axelrod.

Opposite, upper photo:
The hellbender, *Cryptobranchus alleganiensis*, can give a nasty bite when handled improperly. This very slippery animal can be caught by grabbing it at the neck and at the same time holding on to the front legs. Photo by Dr. Sherman A. Minton.

Opposite, lower photo:
Sirens, having no hind legs and only very tiny front legs, can be easily confused with eels. A close examination, however, will show the presence of external gills. The lesser siren, *Siren intermedia*, is shown here. Photo by Dr. Sherman A. Minton.

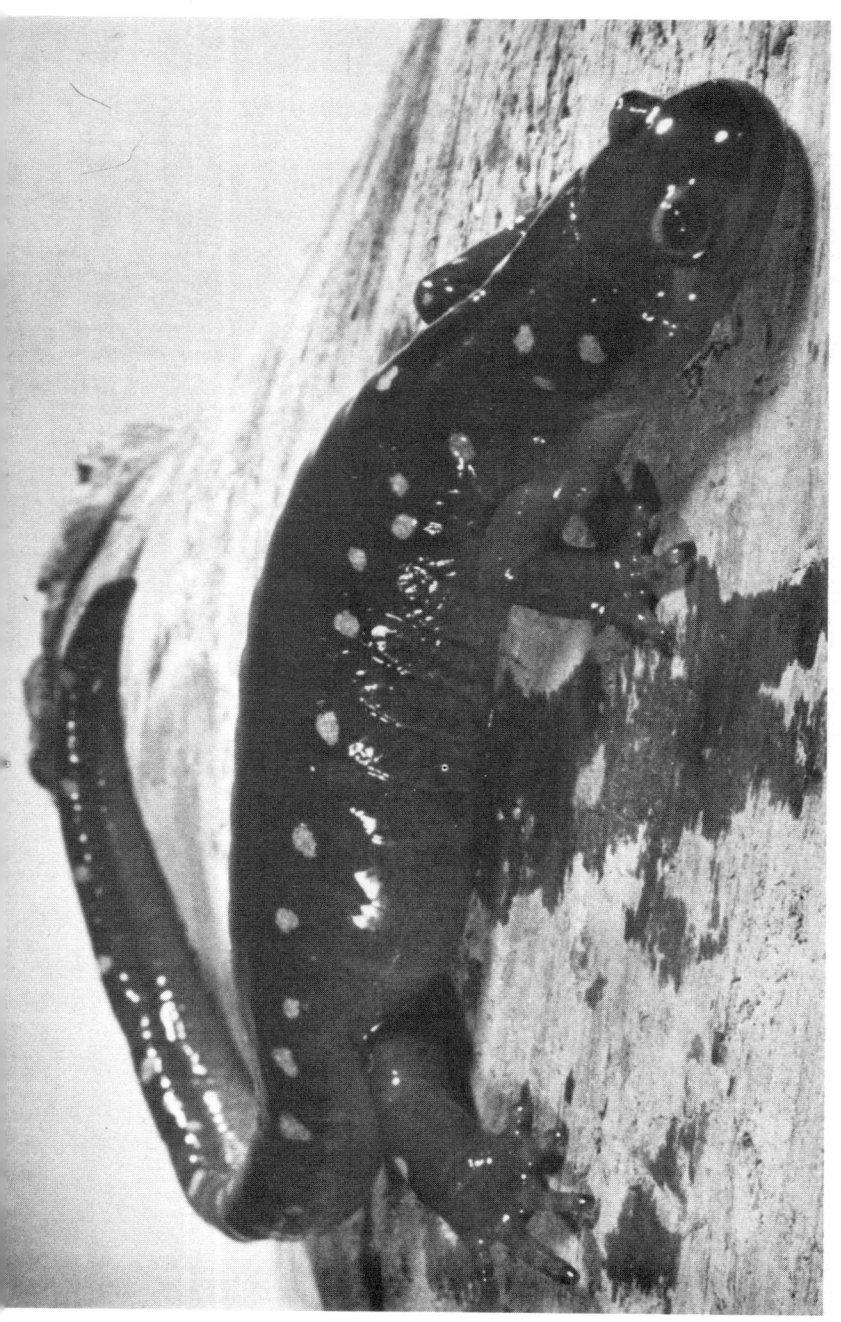

The spotted salamander, *Ambystoma maculatum*, is a common representative of the family Ambystomidae. Mole salamanders, as they are called because of their secretive behavior, occur in the continental U.S. and in certain areas of Canada and Mexico.

What is a Salamander?

The English language is just old enough to have accumulated some words which no longer relate to common usage. "Salamander" is one such word. Synonyms of the past include gnome, sylph, nix and undine. In case you have forgotten, "undine" appears in the mythology of northern Europe and was more recently a heroine of an 1811 romantic novel by Baron Freidrich H.K. De la Motte Fouque (1777-1843). In this most popular story of that period, Undine was cast in her role of an elemental water spirit. She had a form but lacked a soul.

Sir Huldbrand fell in love with Undine (who had assumed the body of a fisherman's daughter) and they were married. On the way to his castle they met Bertalda and took her along. As luck would have it, Huldbrand took up with Bertalda and neglected Undine who left but did not forget. Finally, when Sir Huldbrand was to marry Lady Bertalda, she became thirsty and ordered that a well be unsealed for some special water. Undine escaped from the well and gave her ex-husband a fatal kiss. So there you have it—Salamander—Undine—a fabled female water spirit. And if you don't quite have it—Bertalda was actually the *true* changeling daughter of the fisherman; Undine had swapped places with her.

In still another language difficulty, salamanders were reputed by ancient alchemists to have the ability

The alpine newt, *Triturus alpestris*, is a coldwater species which can even withstand to a limited extent subfreezing temperatures. It is not strictly alpine in distribution, but is a common and widely distributed newt of Europe. The bright uniformly orange belly is characteristic of this species. Seven subspecies are recognized today. Photo by R. Guyetant.

to withstand fire, and although this is not true, the idea persists in the language so that nowadays a stove used by the construction trades to keep the chill off curing concrete or plaster is called a salamander.

Newts fare better in our language. When we say "newt" today we mean a tailed amphibian. This word was derived from "ewt" and eventually "an ewt" became "a newt." Years ago the word "newt" also meant lizard, but that is really quite close by comparison with the problems we have had with the salamander. The difference between a newt and a salamander is not scientific or precise but generally when we loosely speak of newts we mean those salamanders which are smaller, rougher skinned and more apt to be aquatic. Technically all newts are salamanders.

The name game is important for certain scholarly pursuits but this is a book for pet keepers who wish to keep newts and other salamanders. For those students who wish to put together the whole ball of wax, all the *amphibia* are relatively simple. This class (*AMPHIBIA*) contains three orders—SALENTIA also called ANURA (frogs and toads), CAUDATA (newts and other salamanders, and GYMNOPHIONA (caecilians). It is the smallest in number of species of the vertebrate animals, and the newts and other salamanders make up only about 11% of that!

There are world wide perhaps 3000 to 3100 amphibian species, of which about 2400 are frogs and toads (anurans). Additionally, there are between 170 and 320 or so legless worm-like creatures (caecilians) of interest to few other than scientists.

Readers may wonder how it is possible that there are "between 170 and 320 or so" species if they are already known to science. The answer is simple. It depends on whose book you read. Gorham's 1970 checklist gives us 172 species. Taylor in 1969 suggests

320. Gilboa in 1974 says there are 33 genera with 152 species. Fortunately for all of us, salamanders are better known. Hopefully.

To put newts and salamanders in their place is not too difficult. To pin down a few specific details will probably lead to questions best left to taxonomists. Here then, in general terms, is an arrangement which has been simplified to introduce the subject without unduly muddying the waters.

Kingdom — ANIMALIA — Animals.

Phylum — CHORDATA — With a dorsally located central nervous system.

Class — AMPHIBIA — Classically, a double life, part in water, part on land. Actually there are some AMPHIBIA which never go into the water. Lacking scales, hair or feathers.

Sub-class — LISSAMPHIBIA — All modern forms, and some extinct forms.

Order — CAUDATA — Tailed amphibians, omitting caecilians.

I Suborder — CRYPTOBRANCHOIDEA — Primitive forms. Two families.

II Suborder — SIRENOIDEA — Sirens. Sometimes called MEANTES. One family.

III Suborder — SALAMANDROIDEA — Commonly called salamanders. Three families. Some authorities take out one of the three families of SALAMANDROIDEA (PROTEIDAE), and place it in a separate suborder, PROTEOIDEA, consisting of the same two genera shown here for that family.

IV Suborder — AMBYSTOMATOIDEA — New World salamanders. Two families.

Now, within these four suborders with the Roman numerals, we find our subjects—the eight families of tailed amphibians.

This is either a female or an immature *Triturus cristatus*. Both males and females are sexually mature at the age of three years. Egg-laying occurs in the month of April. Photo by Hilmar Hansen.

Opposite, upper photo:
A high and denticulate dorsal crest is developed only in the males of the crested newt, *Triturus cristatus*, during the breeding season. The cloaca also enlarges during this stage.

Opposite, lower photo:
In a non-breeding crested newt the dorsal crest is scarcely noticeable. The white median stripe on the tail is a feature of all male adults. The wart-like growths on the body are mucous glands responsible for the secretion of slime which protects the skin from drying upon exposure to the air. Photo by Dr. Karl Knaack.

SUBORDER CRYPTOBRANCHOIDEA
The Primitive Salamanders
1. Family Hynobiidae. Asian. Five genera.
2. Family Cryptobranchidae. One from Asia and one from North America. Giants. Two genera.

SUBORDER SIRENOIDEA
The Sirens (Meantes)
3. Family Sirenidae. Sirens. Permanently larval and lacking rear legs. Two genera, both from North America.

SUBORDER SALAMANDROIDEA
Northern Hemisphere Salamanders
4. Family Salamandridae. *All* the newts are here and some salamanders also. Nine genera.
5. Family Proteidae. Waterdogs, mudpuppies and olms. Three common names but only two genera. Confusing, but not important unless you are an olm.
6. Family Amphiumidae. Congo eels. Single genus.

SUBORDER AMBYSTOMATOIDEA
New World Internally Fertilized Salamanders
7. Family Ambystomatidae. Mole salamanders. Four genera.
8. Family Plethodontidae. Lungless salamanders. About two dozen genera.

So this is a book about the 326 or so species of the 50 or so genera of the eight families of the four suborders of the order CAUDATA. Fifty years ago CAUDATA was called URODELA and many textbooks still use this older name. Let's take a closer look at them.

Some caudates are rough skinned and others are slimy. None are scaly. None have poisonous bites but several of the larger species can inflict knife type lacerations with their sharp teeth. Some of these CAUDATA have skin glands which release a distasteful or positively poisonous liquid which discourages other animals from eating them. With few exceptions the adult forms are entirely carnivorous and eat only animal food: insects, crustacea, worms, mollusks, fish, other amphibia, etc. In some species the larvae may eat some vegetable matter if there is insufficient animal food available.

The entire class AMPHIBIA range in size from one inch to five feet and in weight from perhaps one-twentieth of an ounce to an absolute maximum of 100 pounds, a factor of no more than 32,000 between the lightest and the heaviest species. The entire class of mammalian species vary in weight from a shrew to a blue whale, say 1/10 ounce to 100 tons, a factor of 32,000,000.

Several salamanders are so rare as to be on the endangered species lists and others are so common as to be readily available to any ten-year-old boy who is willing to turn stones in wet places.

This book will not attempt to describe or even list all of the approximately 326 species but it will help you to recognize all the families and a few representative genera and species. *The emphasis in this book is on keeping them alive in captivity.*

Identification is best accomplished with field guides and these are mentioned in the selected list of references. It should be mentioned that positive identification of many species common in the eastern U.S. is difficult and time consuming. Descriptions of the approximately 70 to 100 U.S. species and subspecies or varieties found east of the 100th meridian, for example, would take up nearly 120 pages of a book like this.

The field guides are arranged with many illustrations on a single page and these illustrations emphasize the differences which aid in identification. No collector of native species should be without a field guide and a check list as well. The check list becomes the key for further investigation.

Two views of an alpine newt, *Triturus alpestris*, photographed in an aquarium. Photos by Stanislav Frank.

Another well known newt from Europe is the palmate newt, *Triturus helveticus*. This species has very finely granulated skin. Males are also distinct from the females, developing a crest and webbed hind legs during the mating season. Photo by Dr. P. Juster.

Since identification sometimes requires counting and measuring toes, one should take care to assure that the specimen is not in the process of regenerating a lost toe. Herpetologists use a formula for noting the length of digits and the arrangement is simple. The first number refers to the front foot and then after the /, the number refers to the hind foot. The digits in the number refer to the length of each toe reading from the inside to the outside and counting from the shortest to the longest. For example, using this system in a human the numbers would likely be 13542/54321. The thumb (1) (inside front foot) is shortest and the "pinkie" (2) is next shortest, followed by the index finger (3) then the ring finger (4) and finally in length the middle finger (5). Then after the diagonal slash the big toe is often the longest and so on. There are on salamanders, it might be mentioned, never normally more than four toes per front foot or more than five per rear foot. The "four-toed salamander" has but four toes on each foot.

FAMILIES

(1) HYNOBIIDAE are primitive Asiatic salamanders. There are five genera. In some species the female enters the water only to lay her masses of eggs. The male then fertilizes the eggs and guards them until they hatch several months later. Other species in this family are denizens of mountain streams. This is a cold water family. They grow slowly and perhaps three years elapse before the aquatic juveniles metamorphose and come up on land. HYNOBIIDAE are rarely available to collectors in the U.S.A.

(2) The family CRYPTOBRANCHIDAE are the giant salamanders of the U.S., Japan and China. The American example is the hellbender of the streams of the Appalachian Mountains and western streams feeding the Mississippi as well. *Cryptobranchus alleganien-*

sis grows to 29 inches and is generally considered to be the most ugly of the CAUDATA. It is unique in America as the only salamander with a slimy, wrinkled, loose skin. It is not poisonous. There are normally paired gill slits or sometimes just one gill slit (on the left side) but no external gills in the adult. The color is blotched brown. Hellbenders are found in moving water, not swimming but crawling over the bottom. Fishermen catch them on hooks. Hellbenders are known to eat small fish, crayfish and worms. A nest is built, the female lays as many as 450 eggs and the male then fertilizes and subsequently guards them. Frequently the underwater nest is a burrow under a rock.

William T. Hornaday in his classic, *The American Natural History*, Scribners, New York, 1914, notes an experience with a hellbender by a Mr. William Frear in which an 18-inch specimen was exposed on the ground to summer sun for two days and then brought to a museum where it was left lying for another day before being placed in alcohol. After twenty hours in the alcohol, it was removed for study and when it was placed on a table, it opened its mouth, vigorously swayed its tail and gave other undoubted signs of vitality. At least one reviewer of *this* book doesn't believe it ever happened; but Hornaday's book was written in 1914 and perhaps they just don't make them like that anymore!

The Oriental giant salamander is *known* to grow to a length of five feet and is sometimes *reputed* to achieve a weight of nearly one hundred pounds. They are desirable as food in Japan and are rare and endangered today. The 100 pound figure sometimes mentioned in other books is probably an exaggeration. Dr. Richard G. Zweifel points out that a hellbender enlarged to 100 pounds would be about eleven feet long.

(3) The family SIRENIDAE contains but two genera, *Siren* and *Pseudobranchus*. The greater siren of

A close relative of the crested newt but with a more restricted range of distribution is the marbled newt, *Triturus marmoratus*. Its green and black color pattern makes it one of the most attractive *Triturus* species. The species is found in Portugal, Spain, and France. Photo by Dr. J.K. Langhammer.

In general, newts such as these *Notophthalmus viridescens* can withstand reasonable handling. There is very little chance that the animal will lose its tail or limbs. Photo by John Dommers.

The spots characteristic of the red-spotted newt, *Notophthalmus viridescens viridescens*, are present not only in the adult and larval stages but also during the eft stage shown here. Photo by Dr. Sherman A. Minton.

southeastern states has no rear legs and its ever-present gills are green; not grass green, but more green than red. This greater siren, *Siren lacertina*, is slate grey with yellow blotches and a markedly keeled tail. It looks like an eel but with external gills and two tiny front legs with four toes on each leg. It grows to a length of three feet.

The lesser siren, *Siren intermedia*, looks like the aforementioned *S. lacertina* but is only fifteen inches maximum; its gills are more blue than green and the tail is less keeled. It also has four toes on each of its two tiny front legs. The range of this and the greater siren overlap, but the lesser siren is also found in the Mississippi.

Sirens are often found in ponds which dry up seasonally. When this happens the animals dig as deeply as they can into the mud, surround themselves with slime from their own bodies which tends to create a moisture barrier and protect them against additional drying out while they wait. When a siren waits for the wet season, it is said to be estivating, which is akin to hibernation in that the life processes slow down until the environment improves. Here again the males fertilize the eggs after they have been deposited by the female.

In addition to the greater sirens and lesser sirens (genus *Siren*), there are also dwarf sirens which are in another genus (*Pseudobranchus*). The dwarf sirens have but three toes on each of their two front legs. Like the greater and lesser sirens, the dwarf sirens also have external gills throughout their lifetimes, but J.F.D. Frazer in *The Larousse Encyclopedia of Animal Life* (1967, McGraw-Hill) questions whether these gills on the dwarf siren are functional. How "functional" is functional? A shade of gray perhaps. Is this a question for a philosopher or a physiologist?

(4) SALAMANDRIDAE is the family of newts and efts. Rough skinned, small, not a bit slimy or slick, they

are easy to recognize by their skins and size. Many predators will bite or swallow a newt only to reject it instantly. There may be a distasteful substance or poison in the skin.

The newt *Notophthalmus viridescens* (previously known as *Diemictylus viridescens*) is yellow green with red spots above and yellow with black dots below when it is aquatic. A still older name for the genus is *Triturus*. On land, the juvenile (not larva) is orange-red with red spots. Kids in camp find red juveniles after rainstorms in the woods and adults all the time in clearwater ponds and lakes. In some areas the eft stage is omitted and the larvae develop directly into aquatic adults. When this happens the adults sometimes retain some of their external larval gills. The larvae are small and rarely noticed. They are common throughout the U.S. east of the Mississippi. The olive adult is called the newt. The red terrestrial juvenile is called the eft or red eft. The larva (with gills) is wholly aquatic for two or three months. The adult newt (with lungs) remains in water permanently. The efts are up to three inches long and the newts range between three and four and a quarter inches. There are three species currently recognized.

The western U.S. newts are another genus, *Taricha*. These lack the eft stage. The land forms eat live insects. Mealworms, fruitflies, house flies, earthworms, and enchytrae (whiteworms) should be tried, for starters. The water forms will eat *Daphnia*, insect larvae, earthworms, *Tubifex* worms and flies which walk on the surface of the water (like "wingless" [vestigial winged] fruit flies).

Taricha, *Notophthalmus*, *Cynops* and *Paramesotriton* are genera known to have poisons in their skin which either discourage or possibly even kill their enemies. More about this in the chapter on toxins.

(5) PROTEIDAE, the mudpuppies, sometimes

The red eft, as the eft stage of the red-spotted newt is known, can be found in moist areas of the eastern United States from Michigan to Florida. Photo by F.J. Dodd.

Frog eggs are commonly eaten by newts in their habitat. Photo by Charles O. Masters.

Two views of the rough-skinned newt, *Taricha granulosa*. Although not strictly aquatic in its natural habitat, this newt can be kept in an aquarium with no apparent harm. The genus *Taricha* is found only in the western part of North America, from British Columbia to California. Photos by J.A. Cavalier.

This is the unique European olm or blind salamander, *Proteus anguinus*. The single species of *Proteus* is very restricted in its habitat and range, being found in underground waters in the extreme southern end of Austria to Yugoslavia. Photo courtesy of the American Museum of Natural History.

called waterdogs, is a New World family with four limbs, each limb having four toes. The olm of the Old World is also in this family. Mudpuppies have three pairs of red or maroon feathery external gills. These gills are retained for life, and of course are totally aquatic. The mudpuppy *Necturus maculosus* grows to seventeen inches and is a drab gray-brown or olive-brown and sometimes spotted. When the external gills are large, they suggest that *Necturus* is prepared to survive where the oxygen content is low, and this is true since mudpuppies are often found in muddy and stagnant waters. In clean cool waters, the gills invariably are smaller. Mudpuppies range throughout the entire Mississippi River system, the southeast, and into the northeastern U.S., including much of the Connecticut River Valley.

Zoology teachers use mudpuppies and waterdogs for classroom and laboratory demonstrations. All the species are hardy and can tolerate a wide range of temperatures.

Proteus, the olm of Europe, is frequently mentioned as an unpigmented blind cave salamander which has been known to survive for over a year without food. It has four limbs with three fingers on the forelegs and four toes on the rear. Adults reach eleven inches in length.

(6) There is but a single genus in the family AMPHIUMIDAE, and it stands out like a sore thumb. These are the congo eels or lamper (*not* lamprey) eels. Those of us who accept Darwin believe that *Amphiuma* evolved from a form with better developed limbs, and all that remains are four tiny vestigial limbs. Congo eels grow to a length of forty inches. Within the one genus there are three species, *Amphiuma pholeter* (the one-toed amphiuma), *Amphiuma means* (the two-toed amphiuma), and *Amphiuma tridactylum* (the three-toed amphiuma). One-toe is found in northern Florida and Georgia; the two-toe is found in the southern coastal states east of the Mississippi, while the three-toe is found in the lower Mississippi Valley.

Amphiuma are almost completely aquatic, but their respiration is accomplished with lungs. There are no gills, but one gill cleft remains open on each side. The male builds a nest and the female deposits her eggs in it, then the male fertilizes the eggs by emitting sperm over them. This breeding is accomplished out of water and the 150 eggs or so are guarded by the female who coils herself around the clutch. Since these animals are bottom crawling, lunged creatures, they should be housed in shallow tanks so as to be able to reach the surface for air without swimming. It is only during breeding that they leave the water. When the young hatch, their lungs are already functional.

These animals should be handled only with a net or heavy gloves. They can inflict a surprisingly dangerous bite with their razor sharp teeth. *Amphiuma* have small eyes and poor vision; bright light seems to make them *really* nasty. Charles Sullivan reports that they do

The tiger salamander, *Ambystoma tigrinum*, is a very widely distributed species in the United States. They are so plentiful that in some parts of the West they are used as fish bait. Photo by Hilmar Hansen.

Distribution and size of the spots in this subspecies of tiger salamander, *Ambystoma tigrinum velasci*, are quite distinct from that of the several other subspecies. Photo by Dr. Sherman A. Minton.

A pair of *Ambystoma tigrinum* larvae. Very large aquarium fish should not be kept with them. The introduction of fish in their natural habitat has resulted in the extinction of entire populations of tiger salamanders. Photo by Ruda Zukal.

Except for the two pairs of very tiny legs, *Amphiuma means* truly resembles the shape of an eel. They are large salamanders commonly reaching a length of 30 inches and as much as 40 inches has been recorded. Photo by F.J. Dodd.

settle down in captivity and feed readily. He kept one for more than seven years.

Food includes anything small enough to swallow including but not limited to frogs, crayfish, small fish and worms. In captivity they will eat strips of raw beef but this should be supplemented with whole organisms and animals with bones to assure an adequate supply of calcium.

(7) The AMBYSTOMATIDAE are a family of slimy, blunt-mouthed, stout-bodied salamanders that have large fleshy tongues. Their larvae have external gills—big bushy gills which disappear during metamorphosis. The adults have lungs and use them since they are terrestrial except when they are breeding. The more common U.S. species are:

Ringed salamander, *Ambystoma annulatum*. Burrows in mud. Missouri, Arkansas, and Oklahoma. Grows to eight inches. Toes 1423/15234.

Jefferson salamander, *Ambystoma jeffersonianum*. Gray to brown with blue spotted sides. Seven inches. Northeastern U.S. Toes 1423/15234.

Spotted salamander, *Ambystoma maculatum*. Two rows of round large yellow spots on a blue-black back. Eight inches, stout. All U.S. east of the Mississippi except Florida. Terrestrial except when breeding. Toes 1423/15234.

Marbled salamander, *Ambystoma opacum*. Smaller than the aforementioned, it grows to only 4½ inches. Shiny black with irregular white bands. Toes 1423/15234. While others of the *Ambystoma* family breed in springtime, this species breeds in the fall. Eastern U.S., except New England and southern Florida.

Mole salamander, *Ambystoma talpoideum*. Stout gray brown with blue dots; from southeast U.S. except southern Florida. Only 3¾ inches long. Toes 1423/15234 or /15243.

Small-mouthed salamander, *Ambystoma texanum*. Six inches with small mouth and slender head. Toes like mole salamander above. Color variable blotchy. White marks below eyes and lower side of tail.

Tiger salamander, *Ambystoma tigrinum*. A ten-inch salamander with yellow blotches on a dark background above and yellow with black marbling below. This is the classical textbook example of metamorphosis after breeding in the larval form (neoteny). There are five or six subspecies in the U.S. This animal is common over most of the U.S. except the high Appalachians and the far southwest and southern Florida. It is a burrower and goes to water only to breed. The adults have the colors described above and their respiration is with lungs. Around Mexico City a larval form is the Axolotl and if it is kept in a drier habitat it will adapt and become the

Ambystoma mexicanum, a close relative of *Ambystoma tigrinum*, usually remains permanently in the larval stage as the Mexican axolotl. Photo by Dr. Sherman A. Minton.

Ambystoma jeffersonianum is a common blackish salamander in the north-central U.S. Photo by Dr. Sherman A. Minton.

The marbled salamander, *Ambystoma opacum*, is a widespread and common eastern U.S. mole salamander. Photo by John Dommers.

Ringed salamanders, *Ambystoma annulatum*, occur mostly in the Ozark Mountains and are seldom seen except when laying eggs. Photo by Dr. Sherman A. Minton.

This frontal view of the head of a cave salamander, *Eurycea lucifuga*, shows very clearly the nasolabial grooves extending from the nostrils to the upper lip. These grooves are often more prominent in males. Only the plethodontids possess such structures. Photo courtesy of the American Museum of Natural History.

rather common tiger salamander. Toes: 3241/43251.

(8) PLETHODONTIDAE, the family of lungless salamanders. These salamanders hatch from eggs laid in water and the larval young retain gills in some species, become aquatic without gills in other species. Still others become terrestrial skin breathers for their adult lives. Many species are found in Appalachian humid mountain forests and streams. Other PLETHODONTIDAE are found in Europe.

There are about two dozen genera and two of these genera in particular, the dusky and the shovelnosed salamanders, *Desmognathus* and *Leurognathus*, are a real challenge for a herpetologist to identify with certainty. Species seem to intergrade and locations of capture may be more important than colors or color patterns.

An expert can, by examining the roof of the mouth, separate the dusky from the shovelnosed. To accomplish this he must pry the mouth open, taking care not to break or dislocate any bones. Then he must separate the jaws one from another rather than bend either from its position relative to the rest of the body. Many of these salamanders open their mouths by raising the head rather than lowering the lower jaw. They have movable upper jaws. Once the jaws are opened wide, he must take a look at the roof of the mouth. In dusky salamanders (*Desmognathus*) the internal openings of the nostrils are clearly visible, approximately in line with the eyes. In the shovelnosed species, he will find that there are no *visible* openings since they are hidden by folds in each side of the roof of the mouth.

The woodland salamanders, genus *Plethodon*, are found in damp forests all over North America. They are truly predatory, even eating stinging ants and hard shelled or smelly bugs. The eggs are laid in damp places and the larval stage is completed before hatching. There are eleven species mostly east of the Mississippi and about ten western forms.

Hydromantes genei is an unusual salamander; it is the only representative of the often cave-dwelling genus *Hydromantes* found outside of the western United States. They are nocturnal and terrestrial plethodontids. Photo courtesy of the American Museum of Natural History.

Ambystoma macrodactylum, an often brightly colored species from the Pacific Northwest of the United States and Canada. Photo by Dr. Sherman A. Minton.

Opposite:
Head and dorsal views of the common spotted salamander, *Ambystoma maculatum*. It resembles a tiger salamander from above except that the yellow spots in the spotted salamander form regular rows and do not extend to the sides of the body or the belly. Upper photo by John Dommers, lower photo by Dr. James K. Langhammer.

Caudate Characteristics

As you read this book, especially the chapter entitled "EXCEPTIONS," it will be apparent that within the caudates there is diversity. True, none fly or sing, but several do jump and a few do bark or squeal. Now that the general disclaimer has been recorded, let's look at what many of them do and how they do it.

They do it slowly. None swims as fast as a fish. They use their tails when swimming and hold their legs in close. They creep with a curious pace-like waddle. It is not a pace, but it certainly looks curious.

The legs of the males of some species are modified during breeding so that the male may better clasp his mate. Among the European mountain brook newts (*Euproctus*) the male snares the female with his prehensile tail and holds her so tightly that sometimes he squeezes her to death.

When salamanders actively hunt their prey they do it slowly and deliberately. This works fine for fish eggs, frog and toad eggs, their own eggs, pill bugs, worms, termites, *Daphnia* and aphids. When they hunt faster moving prey—for example, hellbenders feeding on fish —they accomplish their ends by stealth. Nothing moves rapidly except the lower jaw. They gulp and seem to suck in their prey with the water—as catfish also seem to do.

Some terrestrial forms have sticky tongues. Some have tongues which extend beyond their lips and others do their initial grasping with their teeth.

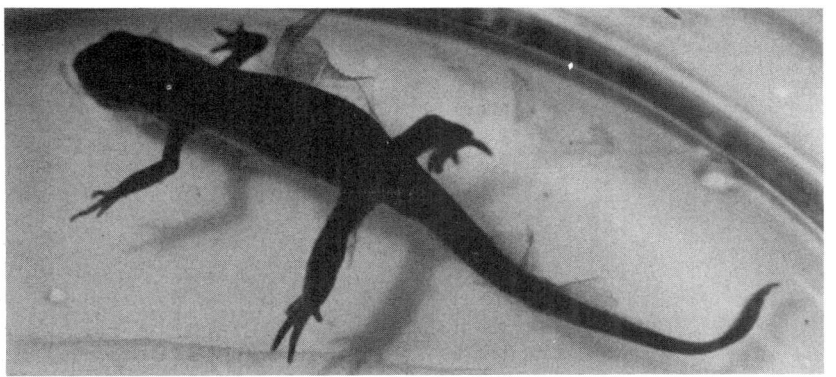

A salamander shedding off portions of its skin. Only the outermost layer of the epidermis consisting of almost transparent, flattened cells, is shed. Photo by John Dommers.

Males dance, secrete perfumes and intensify their colors to attract females. More about odors later on.

Some adults guard eggs but none demonstrate any great parental care of their young. *Hemidactylium* and *Plethodon* may stay with their young for a while after hatching, but if true, that's the extent of it.

Many have poisonous or distasteful skins or skin secretions. Some can make their skin color change but not as dramatically as tree frogs or chameleons.

The skin also serves some species as a respiratory apparatus which suffices alone or in conjunction with other modes of oxygen/carbon dioxide exchange. Gills exist in some larvae and in permanently larval forms, and, in others, there are lungs, while in still others the exchange is effected by buccopharyngeal respiration—a matter of fluttering the floor of the mouth to move air across the moist blood laden tissues.

From time to time caudates shed their skins. They cast them off much in the way a snake sheds his skin. These thin outer membranes are important since they act as a barrier against parasites and bacteria, also they act as a vapor barrier to keep these scaleless sometimes slimy animals from drying out. When an amphibian

The dusky salamander, *Desmognathus fuscus*, comes in many color patterns and is often very common in the eastern United States. Photo by J.K. Dodd.

Red salamanders, *Pseudotriton ruber*, are often found buried under logs and moss in bogs. Photo by Dr. Sherman A. Minton.

Above, longtailed salamander, *Eurycea longicauda*. Photo by Dr. James K. Langhammer; below, cave salamander, *Eurycea lucifuga*. Photo by Dr. James K. Langhammer. *Eurycea* larvae are often common in small streams, especially in mountainous areas with cool waters containing much oxygen. The adults are common near such streams.

casts his skin he frequently eats it and this is perfectly normal and proper. Sometimes molting is caused by skin injury or hormonal disturbance, and this can happen anytime, regardless of the need to grow.

Since we know that urodeles are mostly silent and some may be color-blind or too stupid to discriminate between colors, we presently think that odor plays a part in bringing the sexes together for breeding and also separating the species.

Odor is important for feeding. We know that *Amphiuma*, for example, eats clams which they would have trouble finding by vision alone.

Newts and other salamanders cannot control their body heat internally, so they cope with the temperature of the air and water by their behavior instead. They search out the temperature they like, and move to remain at the warmth level they like. Some go to deep water to keep from freezing and others burrow below the frostline and then hibernate. According to G.K. Noble some non-tropical species can survive short periods of freezing in solid blocks of ice. In fact, they would probably be more liable to die at the same temperature if they were simply chilled in the open air. Death would probably be due to dehydration.

CAUDATA can and do bite their enemies as well as their foods. Many are able to draw blood from the hands of would-be collectors. *Amphiuma* twists and simultaneously bites when attempts are made to capture it.

Many newt and other salamander species resemble each other so closely as to confuse us humans, but the mommas and the papas seem to work it out. The clue is probably odor, and the human problem is that *we* people probably don't sense certain odors. For one example which we do recognize by its odor, consider the common fire salamander, *Salamandra salamandra* of

Salamanders and newts could bite collectors and handlers just as they bite their food. With some exceptions, the amphiumas for example, their bite is more like a pinch and is harmless. Photo by Hans Pfletschinger.

Europe. It smells, to people, like vanilla.

Ambystoma and *Plethodon*, among others, are known to become immobile when handled. They seem hypnotized or "playing possum." This seems to be a protective device and is also demonstrated by toads, frogs, at least one snake, some birds, and of course the Virginia opossum.

Salamanders are disease resistant, long lived, colorful, easy to feed, inexpensive to house, quiet, relatively odorless, and many can be bred in captivity. They are readily available in many parts of the world and may be purchased in pet shops or from reptile dealers. This book was written by a pet keeper for pet keepers and the main thrust is directed toward the humane and intelligent care of these animals as pets.

The red-backed phase of *Plethodon cinereus* is recognized by the reddish stripe along the back. Photo by John Dommers.

Opposite, upper photo:
Woodland salamanders, like a red-backed salamander, *Plethodon cinereus*, seen here, only venture out of their hiding places at night or after a heavy rainfall. Collecting them requires turning up logs and stones or sifting through dead leaves and debris in forest areas. Photo by John Dommers.

Opposite, lower photo:
In the true lead-backed phase of *Plethodon cinereus* the animals appear uniformly dark gray to black. Shown here is an intermediate between the red-backed and lead-backed phases. Photo by John Dommers.

Exceptions

In Nature, most sweeping generalities are punctuated with exceptions and here is a short list of exceptions which, if not recognized, will make an "expert" feel foolish.

CAUDATA are silent and perhaps deaf. They may pick up some sounds as vibrations through their front feet to the skull. Some exceptions are that the Pacific giant salamanders (*Dicamptodon*) make a low bark or scream when disturbed. *Aneides lugubris* squeaks. Sirens and amphiumas whistle and *Andrias* (*Megalobatrachus*) makes shrill cries.

CAUDATA eggs are fertilized internally without coitus. The male deposits a packet of sperm on a gelatinous base and the female picks it up with the lips of her cloaca and stores it against the time she lays her eggs in water. The exceptions are found with *Andrias*, the giant salamanders of China and Japan, the American sirens and the hellbenders. Here the females lay their eggs in sticky masses on a rock. The egg masses sometimes seem to glue the female to the spot. The male then pushes her aside with his hind feet and distributes his sperm over the glue covered mass to fertilize the eggs.

Another exception to the usual breeding pattern is found in the European fire salamander, *Salamandra salamandra*. Here the male embraces the female by climbing on her back. The eggs mature within the female's body and the young are born alive.

Still another exception is found in the alpine salamander of Europe, *S. atra*. Here the young are born on land rather than hatched from eggs and these young do not go through a larval stage, but are born without gills. The genus *Plethodon* also pass through their gilled larval stages within the egg and emerge looking like their parents.

CAUDATA can regenerate lost appendages, sometimes even eyes, but generally they hang onto their tails even when under stress. One exception to this is the four-toed salamander, *Hemidactylum scutatum*, which has a marked constriction at the base of its tail, and this is the place where an easy break-off occurs.

CAUDATA occur in all colors except green—except for the green salamander, *Aneides aeneus*, which is really green. It is also exceptional in that while other salamanders have tapering toes, this one has square tipped toes.

CAUDATA are aquatic, terrestrial or both (amphibious, i.e., double-life). Exception: *Aneides lugubris* is called the arboreal salamander and is sometimes found in trees to a height of over sixty feet! This is a western U.S. species and is also singular in the determination of the female to defend her eggs by biting. Also there are many tropical American salamanders which are arboreal or partly so.

CAUDATA are *the* tailed amphibians (the caudal fin of a fish, for instance, being its tail). Except: Caecilians and there is a tailed frog, but only the male has a tail and not much of one at that.

CAUDATA are clawless. Exceptions: The Japanese *Onychodactylus japonicus* has sharp curved claws which resemble lizard's claws. Also, the American siren has pointed claw-like caps over the ends of its toes.

CAUDATA are either smooth, or slimy, or rough skinned. Exception: The ribbed newt of Spain, *Pleuro-*

Slimy salamander, *Plethodon glutinosus*. Photo by Dr. Sherman A. Minton.

Opposite, upper photo:
The size and distribution of the body spots or flecks are very variable in *Plethodon glutinosus*. Photo by John Dommers.

Opposite, lower photo:
Ravine salamanders, *Plethodon richmondi*, occur in unusual types of habitat. They prefer to live in wooded slopes and ravines, avoiding hill tops and valley floors. The species is found from Illinois and Indiana to Pennsylvania and south to Tennessee and North Carolina. Photo by Dr. Sherman A. Minton.

The most prominent feature of the ribbed newt from Spain, *Pleurodeles waltl*, is the series of protuberances along each side of the body. Each projection corresponds to the tip of a rib. Such projections presumably help protect this newt from predators. Photo by G. Marcuse.

deles waltl, is blessed with ribs which are pointed and may actually punch through the skin as a row of spines on each side. They probably function as protective devices.

CAUDATA swim and/or crawl, everyone knows that. Several also climb trees. Except: Several leap. They leap at least their body length. They jump certainly to escape enemies and possibly also to capture food. Charles Sullivan notes that the *Desmognathus* and especially *D. wrighti* are particularly noted for their leaping ability.

Longevity

There is an established record for a Japanese giant salamander which is known to have lived 52 years in Leyden, the Netherlands. This zoo captive was believed to have been at least three years old when it arrived, so its age at death was probably 55 years. Sirens, axolotls, amphiumas and hellbenders have all passed the 25 year mark in captivity.

Species from cold climes and those which hibernate probably live longer than species from warmer habitats. Individuals in captivity should be expected to do better than their wild siblings if only because they are protected from predators. The common red eft sometimes spends two or even three years on land before it returns to the water for the remainder of its adult life—perhaps another three to five years—as the red spotted newt so popular with pet keepers.

The following records have been established for CAUDATA in captivity:

Japanese giant salamander,
    Andrias (Megalobatrachus) maximus   52 years
Fire salamander,
    Salamandra salamandra   40 years
Two-toed amphiuma,
    Amphiuma means   26 years
Japanese newt,
    Triturus (Cynops) pyrrhogaster   25 years

Note the unusually well developed limbs of this clouded salamander, *Aneides ferreus*, one of the species found on the Pacific coast. The genus *Aneides* contains tree-climbing and cliff-dwelling salamanders. These salamanders are also noted for their powerful jaws. Photo by Dr. Sherman A. Minton.

The arboreal salamander, *Aneides lugubris*, is another well known tree climber from the west coast. This particular specimen was taken in the San Francisco Bay area. Photo by Dr. Sherman A. Minton.

Salamanders can be fed the many species of small and large flies and insect larvae found in moist surroundings. Craneflies and their larvae are often abundant in moist woods inhabited by *Plethodon*. Photo by Charles O. Masters.

It is not surprising that salamanders and newts live so long on account of their secretive habits and inactive mode of life. Many estivate during the dry parts of the year. Photo by G. Marcuse.

Sirens,
    Siren species   25 years
Spanish newt,
    Pleurodeles waltl   20 years
Alpine newt,
    Triturus alpestris   20 years

Larger Collections

Throughout the U.S. many species are readily available to "hobby collectors" who simply visit a stream or a bog or a woodland glen and turn logs and stones. For readers who cannot find all the types that interest them near their homes, here is a list of CAUDATA available for sale from time to time.

It should be remembered that living animals like these cannot be kept on the shelf indefinitely while waiting for a customer. Stocks will vary with seasons and sometimes with the rainfall. During the period 1973-1975 the prices for native American species ranged from less than one dollar each for some newts and other small salamanders to $35 for a large hellbender suitable for public display. Your pet shop is the best place to order or buy any salamander or newt.

The following price list is typical and is used here only as an example. Prices vary widely and you must remember that packing and shipping charges must be added to these prices.

CRYPTOBRANCHIDAE, AMPHIUMA AND SIRENIDAE

Hellbender, *Cryptobranchus alleganiensis*, $35.00; two-toed amphiuma, *Amphiuma means*, $6.00-20.00; three-toed amphiuma, *Amphiuma tridactylum*, $6.00-20.00; greater siren, *Siren lacertina*, $4.00-20.00; eastern lesser siren, *Siren i. intermedia*, $4.00; western lesser siren, *Siren i. nettingi*, $6.00; dwarf siren, *Pseudobranchus striatus*, $4.00; mudpuppy, *Necturus maculosus*, $7.50.

The Plethodontidae, the largest family of salamanders, is (except for the species of *Hydromantes* found in Italy and Sardinia) confined to the new world. Representatives extend as far south as the northern parts of South America. Shown here are some *Pseudoeurycea* species from Mexico. All photos by Dr. Sherman A. Minton.

Above:
Pseudoeurycea cephalica, from Hidalgo.

Opposite, upper photo:
Pseudoeurycea belli, from the Oaxaca Mountains. This is a very colorful and widespread species in Mexico. Like most pseudoeuryceas, it is typically a montane species.

Opposite, lower photo:
Pseudoeurycea sp. (near *scandens*), from Pinal de Amoles. Note the stub-like toes of this salamander. Many Central and South American salamanders show a strong tendency to develop strong webs between the often shortened toes.

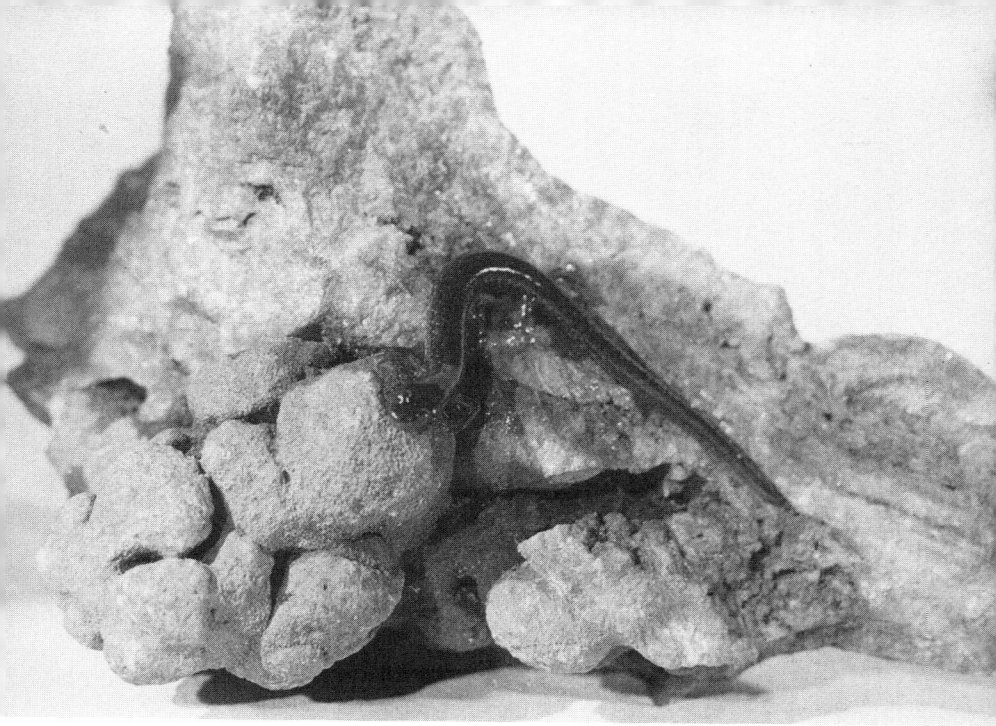

The number of costal grooves (folds on the sides of the body between the front and hind legs) in the many-ribbed salamander, *Eurycea multiplicata,* are important for the identification of this and many other species. Photo courtesy of the American Museum of Natural History.

AMBYSTOMIDAE

Jefferson salamander, *Ambystoma jeffersonianum*, $3.50; small-mouthed salamander, *Ambystoma texanum*, $2.50; mole salamander, *Ambystoma talpoideum*, $2.50; neotenic/aquatic mole salamander, *Ambystoma talpoideum*, $4.50; marbled salamander, *Ambystoma opacum*, $2.50; spotted salamander, *Ambystoma maculatum*, $2.50; eastern tiger salamander, *Ambystoma t. tigrinum*, $4.00; barred tiger salamander, *Ambystoma t. mavortium*, $5.00; neotenic/aquatic tiger, *Ambystoma t. mavortium*, $6.00; ringed salamander, *Ambystoma annulatum*, $4.00; frosted flatwoods salamander, *Ambystoma cingulatum*, $5.00.

SALAMANDRIDAE—*Diemictylus* and *Taricha*

Crimson spotted newt, *Diemictylus v. viridescens*, $.35; red eft, *Diemictylus v. viridescens*, $1.00; central newt, *Diemictylus v. louisianensis*, $1.00; striped newt, *Diemictylus perstriatus*, $1.60; broken striped newt, *Diemictylus v. dorsalis*, $1.25; western newt, *Taricha torosa*, $1.25; red-bellied newt, *Taricha rivularis*, $2.25; rough-skinned newt, *Taricha granulosa*, $1.40.

PLETHODONTIDAE—*Desmognathus* and *Leurognathus*

Northern dusky salamander, *Desmognathus f. fuscus*, $1.00; southern dusky salamander, *Desmognathus auri-*

The two-lined salamander, *Eurycea bislineata*, is a typical brook salamander preferring areas along the edge of brooks and springs. Photo courtesy of the American Museum of Natural History.

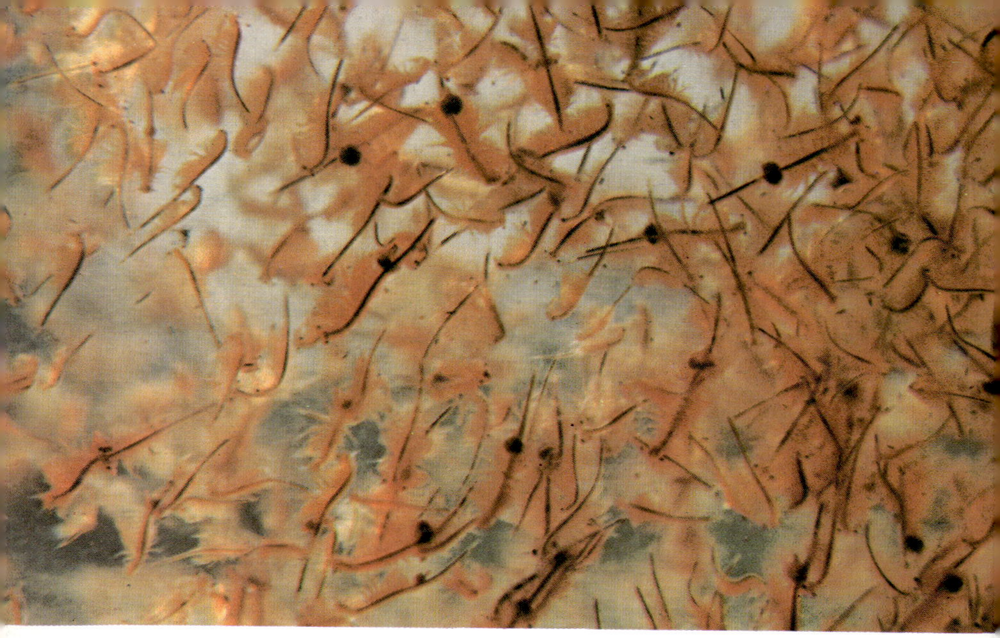

Brine shrimp is great food for small aquatic salamanders and newts. They are easy to maintain alive and not too hard to digest. Just be sure to rinse the shrimp well before feeding. Photo by Charles O. Masters.

Newts and mole salamanders enjoy earthworms. They are quite nutritious being more meaty than most other live foods. Photo by Charles O. Masters.

Salamanders are a simple and enjoyable way for children to learn a little bit about natural history. A spotted salamander is the focus of this boy's interest. Photo by John Dommers.

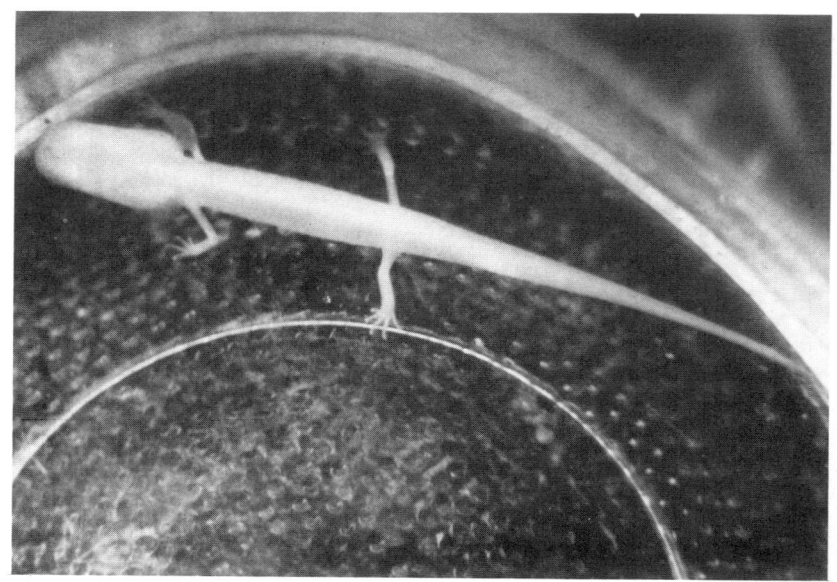

The Georgia blind salamander, *Haideotriton wallacei*, lacks any skin pigmentation and functional eyes. A specimen was recorded taken from a well 200 feet deep, and it has been found in caves in Florida. Photo by F.J. Dodd.

culatus, $2.00; spotted dusky salamander, *Desmognathus f. conanti*, $1.20; mountain dusky salamander, *Desmognathus ochrophaeus*, $.80; imitator salamander, *Desmognathus ochrophaeus*, $2.50; Appalachian seal salamander, *Desmognathus monticola*, $1.50; black-bellied salamander, *Desmognathus quadramaculatus*, $2.00; northern shovelnosed salamander, *Leurognathus m. marmoratus*, $3.00; southern shovelnosed salamander, *Leurognathus m. intermedius*, $3.00.

PLETHODONTIDAE—*Plethodon*

Red-backed salamander, *Plethodon cinereus*, $2.00; zigzag salamander, *Plethodon dorsalis*, $1.50; ravine salamander, *Plethodon richmondi*, $3.00; slimy salamander, *Plethodon glutinosus*, $1.50.

PLETHODONTIDAE—*Hemidactylium* and *Manculus*

Four-toed salamander, *Hemidactylium scutatum*, $2.50; dwarf salamander, *Manculus quadridigitatus*, $2.50.

PLETHODONTIDAE—*Aneides*

Green salamander, *Aneides aeneus*, $3.00; speckled black salamander, *Aneides f. flavipunctatus*, $4.00; clouded salamander, *Aneides ferreus*, $4.00; arboreal salamander, *Aneides lugubris*, $4.00.

PLETHODONTIDAE—*Batrachoseps*

California slender salamander, *Batrachoseps attenuatus*, $2.00; garden slender salamander, *Batrachoseps p. major*, $2.00.

The grotto salamander, *Typhlotriton spelaeus*, has an unusual life-history. The larvae are found in streams and springs outside caves. They return later to the cave to mature and breed. Photo courtesy of the American Museum of Natural History.

For keeping terrestrial salamanders it is best to get moist humus, preferably from their natural habitat, as this child is doing. Some species when placed in water will drown and most will rapidly die if kept too dry. Photo by John Dommers.

Many newts and all other forms with functional gills can only be kept in water. A fish tank is here shown being prepared to house a couple of *Notophthalmus viridescens*. Photo by John Dommers.

The cave salamander, *Eurycea lucifuga*, is an active animal that can be found living either inside or outside caves and old mines. Young individuals have relatively shorter tails. Photo courtesy of the American Museum of Natural History.

PLETHODONTIDAE—*Gyrinophilus* and *Pseudotriton*

Northern spring salamander, *Gyrinophilus p. porphyriticus*, $3.00; Blue Ridge spring salamander, *Gyrinophilus p. danielsi*, $3.00; Carolina spring salamander, *Gyrinophilus p. dunni*, $3.00; northern red salamander, *Pseudotriton r. ruber*, $3.00; black-chinned red salamander, *Pseudotriton r. schenki*, $3.00; southern red salamander, *Pseudotriton r. vioscai*, $4.00; midland mud salamander, *Pseudotriton m. diastictus*, $4.00; rusty mud salamander, *Pseudotriton m. floridanus*, $6.00.

PLETHODONTIDAE—*Eurycea*

Northern two-lined salamander, *Eurycea b. bislineata*, $1.00; southern two-lined salamander, *Eurycea b. cirrigera*, $1.25; Blue Ridge two-lined salamander, *Eurycea b. wilderae*, $2.00; long-tailed salamander, *Eurycea l. longicauda*, $2.50; three-lined salamander, *Eurycea l. guttolineata*, $2.50; cave salamander, *Eurycea lucifuga*, $3.00.

Regeneration

Salamanders have the ability to regenerate parts of their bodies. Cut in half, they surely die, but a lost digit or perhaps even an entire leg or most of a tail or even an eye will be regenerated in time and the new organ or appendage will closely resemble the lost member. This applies to gills as well; if a few pieces are nipped off in a fight you would do well to separate the combatants and increase the oxygen supply. Chances are good that skin respiration will take over immediately and gradually the new gills will grow to function and the specimen will not die for lack of oxygen.

A spotted salamander, *Ambystoma maculatum*, which has lost digits on its right front leg. In time the lost parts may regenerate. Photo courtesy of the American Museum of Natural History.

Housing

Some CAUDATA are aquatic throughout their lives, others are truly amphibious, and still others spend most of their time out of water. Terrestrial forms' habitats are certainly damp but not necessarily immersed. The range of habitat is from wells and caves deep underground to mountain streams at elevations to 11,000 feet, even the upper limbs of rainforest trees. About 75% of CAUDATA are terrestrial.

What they do have in common is a need for moisture. No newt or other salamander will willingly expose itself to direct sunlight for any extended period and all must depend on their environment to keep their skins moist or wet.

You should house your salamanders in jars or aquariums with glass covers. Don't worry about them getting enough air. So long as the cover is not cemented in place, the normal variations in barometric pressure and temperature will assure a constant circulation of air sufficient for their needs. One other thing about the cover. It should be heavy enough to assure that your specimen cannot push it aside or raise it—and if there are small children or household pets in the area, provisions should be made to keep them from uncovering your specimens.

A Japanese giant salamander or an American hellbender can easily live 25 years with minimal care from his owner, but just a few hours behind the radiator and chances are he has had it.

Another aspect of housing your pets is that none requires the elevated temperatures relished by some reptiles and many fishes. The cave dwellers probably do best at 56° F., plus or minus 4° and many species have been seen swimming beneath the ice in ponds and brooks. Normal household temperatures are certainly as high as any species requires and almost all species will do better at even lower temperatures. Always keep them below 75° F. Cold running tap water has been used in many aquarium displays for housing CAUDATA so long as it is not heavily chlorinated. This is especially convenient for large specimens with a big turnover of food and waste products. The small amount of chlorine in some municipal water supplies is usually not enough to hurt these animals. One caution, however, the water department may increase the chlorine and neglect to notify you—*even if you ask them to!*

A heavy duty aquarium water pump with an oversize outside filter is also effective if the filter medium is changed frequently enough to keep from overloading the pump motor. Crowding is the criterion here. Many of these animals are found only in swiftly moving, cool mountain streams and the closer you can approximate this environment, the better off your specimen will fare.

Although some species are found in mud, a mud bottomed aquarium is not especially desirable from the standpoint of observing the animal or keeping the habitat from fouling. The population density of a mud bottomed lake is apt to be much lower than you will be willing to provide for an amphibian in captivity and here is the rub. His food supply is not necessarily all eaten; some will decay. His waste products are not necessarily all completely digested and inert; some of this also will decay. In the pond, bacteria and scavengers take over. In the aquarium the balance is harder to achieve and pollution often results.

Lighting is for your convenience. Newts and other salamanders don't need it; certainly the blind cave dwellers will have to adapt themselves to it. Cave species will become darker if exposed to light. If light is desired, keep it subdued. Certainly, *don't permit the light to generate heat within the container*. Cave dwelling species might do best in darkness and the display lighting could be a deep red, similar to the old style safelight used by photographic processors. Overheated quarters usually result in fungus attacks.

Most CAUDATA are solitary rather than social animals. Except when they are breeding, they are often found apart from each other. Many will fight and, if the sizes are very different, the larger may eat or abuse the smaller. Obviously, if you catch several of the same size together, you can be reasonably sure they are all right to keep together. Plants are attractive and desirable in containers with smaller specimens. Large animals tend to tear up any planting as they root about for food or new hiding places. The plants do not contribute anything to the environment of the container, but they certainly improve its looks. You may, if you wish, call the housing arrangement a terrarium and furnish it with mosses and ferns and install a few red efts and they will surely thrive and prosper in their damp bog-like environment, but generally speaking, the majority of larger aquatic tailed amphibians do as well or better with wood, gravel, and stone furnishings rather than plants and mud.

A lid is *most* important for a reason not mentioned previously, and that is humidity control. Most U.S. homes are much too dry to satisfy a terrestrial specimen and an uncovered tank of water for an aquatic set-up will quickly dry out if it is not fully covered with a glass top. Keep it out of direct sunlight as it will over-heat and kill your pets.

Foods

Most captive wild animals do best on what they would eat if they were free. Since most salamanders are not well equipped to cut or eviscerate their foods, we can assume that their ideal natural intake should be whole organisms. Whole worms should be of a size they can handle or, if necessary, cut up for ease of handling, but with the idea that eventually one specimen will consume some part of every organ in the worm. This goes as well for terrestrial and aquatic insects, crustacea and even the fishes and mice which you might feed to a giant salamander or a large hellbender.

By feeding as much as the animal will eat as frequently as it seems hungry, and by providing variety in fresh or live foods, your pet will probably need no diet supplement. Some zoos with large collections, tight budgets and small staffs like to feed economical "universal" foods on strict schedules. Perhaps too, they would prefer not to risk fouling the cages by overfeeding; so you may find that you will feed your specimens larger quantities with more variety, more frequently. You will witness more growth, may also be more successful with breeding any pairs you own and, of course, you will find it necessary to clean up more frequently.

There are several good books on collecting and propagating live foods for pets. Try reading *Live Foods for Aquarium and Terrarium Animals*, by Jocher, TFH Publications, Neptune City, N.J., or Charles O. Master's *Encyclopedia of Live Foods*, another TFH book.

Small earthworms are a most convenient and easily available food for salamanders and newts. Your daily supply can be retrieved from your own backyard or neighbor's lot. Photo by P. Imgrund.

A short list of suggestions starts with worms and ends with worms. Worms are the salamander keeper's best friends. They are easy to obtain, keep, and most species are simple to rear. They come in many sizes; some terrestrial varieties will survive in water for a few hours. The common earthworm is great for any specimen large enough to grab one end.

Another redworm which you may encounter is the red dungworm found not in garden soils but in manure. This worm has a distinctive musty unpleasant odor which you will learn to recognize and avoid. Most newts and other salamanders will refuse to eat these red dungworms. Earthworms can be purchased from fish bait dealers or you may wish to breed them yourself in an "enriched" mulch pile. *Tubifex* worms are always available at aquarium stores and they are great!

Frog and toad eggs are eaten by some aquatic species and, in season, these are readily available. Newly hatched tadpoles and pollywogs are good food for CAUDATES and are easy to handle. Simply collect the egg mass in its own pond water and let Nature take its course at room temperature and in daylight. As the larvae hatch they can be fed immediately or raised to larger size before offering them to your pets. Virtually all frog and toad larvae are vegetarian.

Crayfish are good food for larger specimens and can be caught or bought in bait stores. Crickets, too, are available from bait dealers. They are inexpensive and easy to propagate. Fishing and hunting magazines frequently carry advertisements for crickets. Remember that crickets can be noisy.

Fruitflies (*Drosophila*) can be cultured in small glass jars and are great for small aquatic and terrestrial salamanders. Starter cultures can be purchased through the mail. Advertisers are found in tropical fish hobbyist magazines.

Whiteworms are available in pet shops and starter cultures can be kept going indefinitely.

Mealworms are sold in pet shops to bird fanciers by the thousand and they too can even be bred by the hobbyist, but they are so cheap it hardly pays to bother. However, they are not recommended as a sole diet.

Respiration

CAUDATA are the transitional vertebrate animals. Within this order of tailed amphibians we find most of the history of animal respiration. There are examples of lung, gill, and cutaneous (skin) respiration. Not only are there salamanders with each of the three modes of respiration, but many species use more than just one mode at the same time and several pass through stages where they change from one to another.

In fact, for many years the axolotl was known to be a large salamander found new Mexico City. It had gills. About the time of the U.S. Civil War, there were several of these rare axolotls (*Ambystoma*) in a zoo in Paris. Eggs were laid and the offspring which hatched out were small gilled copies of their parents. No exclamation point here, but rather just what one would expect. Gilled adults producing gilled young—simple.

Now for the exclamation point: Several of the gilled youngsters lost their gills, changed colors and climbed out of the water! By this time the young transformed axolotls were easily recognizable as tiger salamanders—common in many parts of America. These axolotls, and some other salamanders as well, are actually able to reproduce themselves while they are in their immature or larval form. This was as much of a shock in 1865 as biologists would get today if tadpoles mated, laid eggs and produced more tadpoles. The author knows of nowhere else besides the salamanders and

The skin, a principal or auxiliary respiratory organ of salamanders and newts, is richly supplied with a network of thin capillaries. These blood vessels are clearly visible in this broken-striped newt, *Notophthalmus viridescens dorsalis*. Photo by the author.

some fishes in the vertebrate animal kingdom where there is evidence that a larval form—not the final adult—can reproduce itself.

This arrested development is technically called neotony—*the period of immaturity indefinitely prolonged*. Some termites are known to be able to do it so that they can convert a worker into a queen, but this is a social insect and not a vertebrate. Another technical word for your vocabulary is paedogenesis—*reproduction in the larval state*.

Skin respiration in salamanders permits life in either water or air. In water, the oxygen content must, necessarily, be high to accomplish this, and so it is a mode limited (in water) to inhabitants of fast moving, cold streams since the oxygen carrying capacity of water increases as the temperature goes down.

In air, skin respiration will permit the same animal to continue to prosper with no change in life style so long as the humidity is high. This animal could not leave water for long if he were equipped with external gills. They are too fragile and subject to air drying even in the most humid of atmospheres. Oxygen-carbon dioxide transfer also takes place in the mouth as the animal takes in air and then closes his nostrils and pumps with the floor of his mouth—using it like a diaphragm or bellows on an old style pipe organ. This is called *buccal pumping* and it would be inefficient and insufficient for larger animals with high metabolic rates, but the proof is in the pudding, for some salamanders it works perfectly.

Gill respiration is efficient since the blood is only one cell away from the oxygen in the water, but external gills are vulnerable to attack by animals that might take a nip while passing by. Internal gills, like those found in fishes, require that water flows constantly through the mouth, then finally to exit through gill slits or out the back of the operculum or gill cover. This is adequate for fish which constantly pump water (like a goldfish) or which live in fast moving cold water but less so for slow moving salamanders in ponds.

Lung respiration in salamanders is the third mode and it is similar to that of higher animals except that the air gets to the lungs by the pumping of the floor of the mouth rather than the usual contraction of the diaphragm and the rib cage.

Incidentally, some water turtles also retain the ability to respire through the skin—with them it is in their throats and perhaps their cloacas that the process takes place and permits them (animals with lungs) to remain submerged for extended periods, especially when they are hibernating underwater.

Bear in mind that in polluted water the bacteria have pre-empted the oxygen supply and a gilled amphibian will suffocate. Aquarium water for gilled salamanders must be high in oxygen and low in bacteria and wastes or your specimen is not long for this world.

Reproduction

With the exception of a tree salamander from the west coast of the U.S. which has been heard to squeak when grabbed, most tailed amphibians are silent. The croak of the frog just doesn't happen with salamanders, so they attract each other with odors, dances, and perhaps colors. Some male newts will go through a ritual of rubbing and squirming which will finally culminate

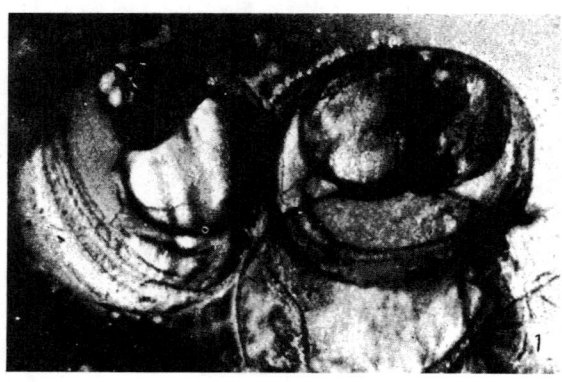

Embryonic *Ambystoma* still enclosed in the egg membrane. Photo by Helmert.

when he released a bundle or packet of sperm which looks like a tiny toadstool or miniature fire hydrant. The female then picks up this spermatophore with the lips of her cloaca and stores it until she is ready to lay her eggs. In other species the male clasps the female with his legs, his digits being modified during the mating season to improve his grip, and again he releases a packet of sperm which she accepts. The packet then dissolves and the sperm cells are stored in her cloaca as previously described. Male hellbenders and sirens simply fertilize the eggs after the female lays them.

A pair of breeding alpine newts, *Triturus alpestris*. The upper (crested) animal is the male. Photo by Gerhard Marcuse.

The ritual of rubbing and squirming varies in detail with the species and may tend to maintain pure stocks of similar species by only exciting females of the same species, but the description of the "X" rated antics of these animals is better left for the more scientific journals.

Some species do reproduce themselves in captivity and the most typical are mentioned in the next chapter.

During the mating season, the males of some newts develop crests along their backs, probably to whip up some enthusiasm from the females. Also, in some species, the color of the males becomes more intense for this month or two once a year.

Breeding in Captivity

Here is a challenge with plenty of unanswered questions. Several species of CAUDATA have been raised from eggs which were laid by captive animals, but the cycle, repeated over and over as it is with many species of fish and all of our domestic animals, is still to be fully mastered. If you should carry your specimens through the entire cycle *and* through several generations *and* then publish your secret, perhaps you will have a claim to fame which your grandchildren will speak of with awe and reverence.

Scientists and students do need a constant supply of freshly laid eggs and metamorphosing young for research and study, make no mistake about that. As time goes on the native populations will be depleted by contamination, loss of the water table and over-harvesting, so it becomes ever more important to establish "domestic" sources of supply for these animals. Erase any thoughts of wealth, but there is a genuine need, and perhaps you can make a contribution.

This effort is now mostly in the hands of academicians in various institutions around the world and they have come a long way, but not quite far enough. How do you start? Bring yourself up to date. Join the American Society of Ichthyologists and Herpetologists (c/o Division of Reptiles, U.S. National Museum, Washington, D.C., 20560). Join the Herpetologists' League (Dept. of Zoology, Tulane University, New Orleans, Louisiana, 70118). Go to your nearest large public library or university library and get professional help to start you in the right direction. Accumulate a library of your own. Read what you can lay your hands on. Today with the wonder of instant reprints, virtually anything in print is available at low cost.

Next, create a hatchery or laboratory—call it what you will. Sunlight is not necessary but a good supply of high quality water and a method of disposing is vital. What kind of water? Low copper, low chlorine, cool water—perhaps ideally, water from a spring where sal-

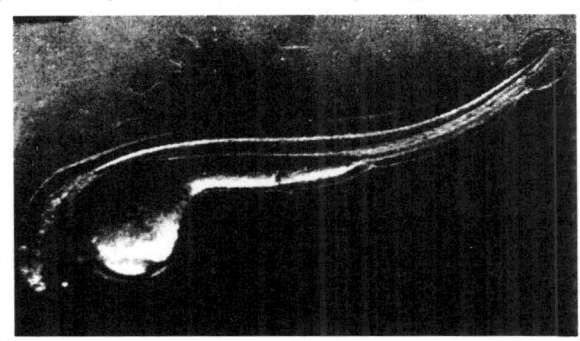

A newly hatched *Ambystoma* larva. With a still non-functional mouth, it depends on the stored food in the yolk sac. Photo by Helmert.

amanders are already established and thriving. This is not as difficult as it sounds because, for example, most of the water in the New York City system comes from areas which support large natural populations of Amphibia. The chlorine, by the time it is delivered to your home, is probably so diluted as to be insignificant and if it isn't, it can be reduced in a holding tank by agitation before passing it into the aquarium with your specimens.

One technique for water quality improvement is to establish a large well planted, well illuminated aquarium, perhaps stocked with a few fish (not Amphibia). The tank should be as large as you can afford and once it is well established with healthy growing plants and a stable population of fish and bacteria, you can draw off as much as one-quarter or one-third of this "acclimated" water two or three times a week for use in the tanks with the Amphibia. This eliminates all the risk of chlorine poisoning.

To control the rate of development of your specimens it might be a good idea to have space available in a refrigerator. Cooling of non-tropical CAUDATA to 50° F. will in most cases slow them down without hurting them. The size of the aquaria is determined by the size of your species, but be cautioned against crowding and against mixing species or sizes.

Crowding leads to cannibalism; the big ones eat the little ones or frighten them into starving to death. Crowding also increases the pollution problems with uneaten food or dead specimens.

Mixing species or sizes causes inhibition of growth, probably through glandular secretions. Many studies have established that large tadpoles, for instance, grow larger and small tadpoles just don't make it—together—but the same small tadpoles if separated will grow and thrive and develop normally even after the period of arrested development. Eventually this inhibiting factor will be isolated and identified and perhaps then it will be found to be associated with claustrophobia in humans, and if this is ever proved, *my* grandchildren will speak of me with awe and reverence!

You should also establish a supply of food for all sizes of the species you choose. This is not expensive, just hard work. The foods you will need to produce should include large paramecia, *Artemia salina* (brine shrimp), *Daphnia, Chironomus,* mosquito larvae, *Drosophila*—both flies *and* larvae, houseflies, white worms, earthworms, crickets and mealworms. You should also be able to obtain and store beef liver, crayfish, canned dog food, and *Tubifex* worms. The *Tubifex* worms thrive in sewers and sewage laden waters and you would be well advised to buy rather than raise or collect your material.

Crayfish are good food with roughage for larger salamanders—hellbenders and sirens, for example—but they are plentiful and more convenient to buy from bait stores than to breed as animal food.

Today the frameless (all glass) aquariums are so inexpensive and reliable that they are far and away the best containers for your captives. One added convenience of all glass frameless aquaria is that they can be sterilized if the need arises, and certainly they are easy to keep clean since there are no dark corners to harbor parasites and predators. The first parasite that comes to mind is the leech and the first predator is the dragonfly naiad. Either could decimate or even wipe out a brood of salamanders in short order.

The animals which already have been mastered or nearly mastered are the Spanish newt, *Pleurodeles waltl*, the Mexican axolotl, *Ambystoma mexicanum*, and to a lesser degree the Japanese newt and the common American newt *Notophthalmus* (*Diemictylus*) *viridescens*.

The American eastern newt (*N. viridescens*), the European common newt (*T. vulgaris*) and their close relatives the crested newt (*T. cristatus*), the palmate newt (*T. helveticus*), and the alpine newt (*T. alpestris*) all have similar habits. These species breed from April through June or July and from 200 to 400 eggs are laid singly on water plant leaves—*Anacharis* (*Elodea*) is frequently the chosen plant, if available. In general, laboratory production of these newts is good for only one generation. When attempts are made to breed the offspring the quality and quantity are disappointing. Perhaps there is a dietary deficiency.

The European fire salamander, *Salamandra salamandra*, produces as many as 40 larvae—each nearly one inch long—from spring to autumn. They mate in water or on land and several months later the female

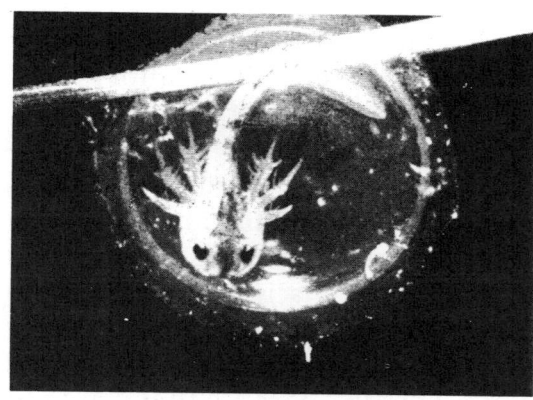

An *Ambystoma* larva actively trying to break out of the egg membrane.

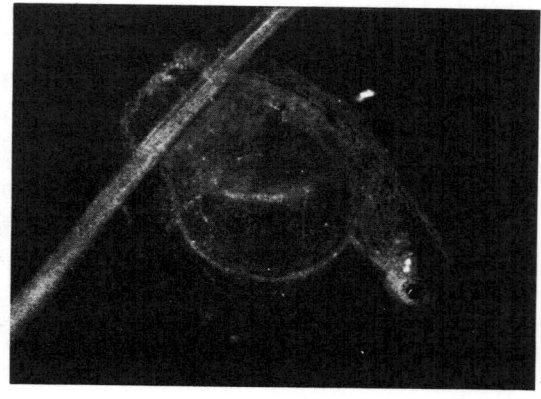

The newly hatched larva slowly moves forward as the sticky egg membrane slides to the rear.

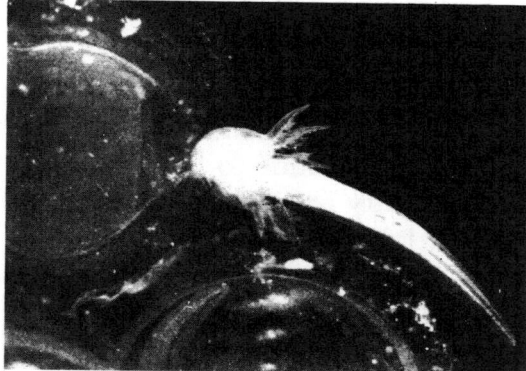

Hatched larvae often cling to the sticky egg remnants for a period of time before swimming freely. All photos by Dr. Knaack.

enters the water to deliver her living young. Sometimes some of the young are still inside sacs but these soon burst and the gilled larvae may take from three to five months to metamorphose. Rarely a female will produce fully metamorphosed (without gills) young which then will be able to live on land immediately. In captivity they have been kept for upwards of 25 years. Suggested foods for large specimens include slugs, crickets, grasshoppers, and of course, earthworms.

The Mexican axolotl (*Ambystoma mexicanum*) adults should be kept singly in gallon containers until they are to be bred. They do well on beef liver and earthworms and will spawn from November to June. The male will place his spermatophore packets in water, on gravel. There may be any number, from one to twenty-five, and the female will begin to spawn her eggs within a day or so after she picks up a packet. She may lay between 300 and 600 eggs in the course of one day. The eggs should hatch in about two weeks and when their yolk sacs are absorbed they should be fed brine shrimp, *Daphnia*, and cut-up *Tubifex* and white worms for starters. As soon as they can handle beef liver they should get it or dietary deficiency diseases may occur. For example, hemorrhage of the small blood vessels in the skin is generally controlled by increasing the red meat component of the diet.

The tiger salamander (*Ambystoma tigrinum*) has done well in captivity. In one reportedly successful procedure the spawned-out adults are transferred to outdoor tanks which approximate their natural environment. They are kept out-of-doors through the entire summer and then placed in a refrigerator at about 40 ° F. until needed for breeding again. Adults could be used this way for three years but apparently the best breeding stock is still caught wild rather than raised in captivity.

Transportation

Tailed amphibians travel easily by air and this is certainly the preferred method. Terrestrial species can be packed loosely in spagnum moss and even skin or lung breathing water dwellers do all right for a few days in wet moss. The gilled species must be in water and to handle them best, you should use "Thermos" or similar vacuum jugs which were first chilled and then filled with cool, clean, filtered water taken from the tanks the animals were in.

Avoid large numbers in one container of water since the death of just one could foul the water and kill the others. Plastic bags inside expanded polystyrene containers—the type used for shipping tropical fish—are excellent and inexpensive. The polystyrene is a good insulator and for one- or two-day trips by air it should do beautifully. Use the *least* quantity of water in the bag for best results.

Several precautions are in order. Your package should be clearly marked "**live animals**" or words to that effect. The freight agent at the airport will help you here. Ask him. The shipment *should not* be made in unpressurized, unheated cargo compartments. When modern jet planes fly at 20,000 feet elevation and outside air temperatures are below zero, your specimens could explode from the rapidly lowered air pressure or freeze from the prolonged exposure to cold even with the insulation you provide.

These Allegheny Mountain salamanders, *Desmognathus ochrophaeus*, are more terrestrial than some other species of dusky salamanders. They should *never* be transported immersed in water for they could easily die by drowning. Photo courtesy of the American Museum of Natural History.

The cost of shipping a styrofoam or cardboard crate the size of a bushel basket and weighing less than ten pounds, including salamanders from, for example, Hartford, Connecticut to Baltimore, Maryland, is only about $12.00. This price would be from airport-to-airport, including taxes.

Shipment of large numbers of salamanders might be facilitated by crowding after lowering the metabolic rate and, of course, the oxygen demand. Anesthetics (tranquilizers) such as MS-222 (Finquel) might be justified but you should discuss this with your veterinarian first, especially since these drugs require a prescription for purchase, and water containing Finquel must be disposed of so as not to tranquilize any other animal life.

Cooling of newts and salamanders to 45° F. is generally sufficient for most shipping situations.

Population Density

Science fiction books to the contrary, newts and salamanders are not about to take over the world, *but* when conditions are right, they can be numerous indeed. In a paper published in *Copeia*, 1975, No. 3, page 541 by Burton and Likens, a study of a salamander population is described. The authors reported that there were about 1,200 salamanders per acre in the Hubbard Brook Experimental Forest of New Hampshire. This works out to a biomass of approximately a pound and a half of newts and other salamanders to the acre. The authors go on to say that this biomass is greater than that of birds during their breeding season (peak density) and is about equal to that of small mammals.

There were five species: the northern dusky salamander (*Desmognathus fuscus fuscus*), the northern two-lined salamander (*Eurycea bislineata bislineata*), the northern (spring) purple salamander (*Gyrinophilus porphyriticus*), the red eft—the land stage of the red spotted newt (*Notophthalmus viridescens viridescens*), and the red-backed salamander (*Plethodon cinereus*).

This study covered the drainage basin of one tiny brook, a total area of about ninety acres. The total summer CAUDATE population was estimated to be over 100,000 individuals of which 70,000 to 85,000 are *P. cinerus*. Of course in addition to the five species of newts and other salamanders there was the normal population of insects, mammals, reptiles, frogs, birds,

The red-backed salamander, *Plethodon cinereus*, appears to be everywhere in most of its range. It can eat a great variety of foods. The life history does not include a larval aquatic stage; the fully developed young hatch directly from eggs laid on land. Photo by F.J. Dodd.

etc. This area under study is somewhat protected against man-made destructive forces but there is no feeding of these animals or other care as would be the case in a zoo. This is just about the normal species distribution and population density of a New England woodland with a brook running through it.

Carrying this a step further, contemplate the number of insects and worms eaten daily by 100,000 salamanders and then visualize the population of insects and worms necessary to supply that much live animal food *every day* for seven or eight unfrozen months of the New Hampshire year. And, for all that, a walk through the woods by a person who didn't know about salamanders would probably reveal few, or more likely none of these little animals.

Toxins

A brief mention of toxicity is found in the introduction, but for the sake of the record and in the hope that it keeps at least one college fraternity pledge from getting sick, it should be mentioned that there are *at least* four genera of Amphibia in the family SALAMANDRIDAE which have had their toxicity measured against the mouse for lethal dose (LD) and the ratings put these creatures in a category which cries for caution. One recent reference is entitled *"Toxicity of the Urodele Amphibians—"* by Brodie, Hensel and Johnson, *Copeia*, 1974, No. 2, pages 506-511. In this paper the toxicity of *Taricha granulosa*, the rough skinned newt from the Pacific Northwest was discussed and the conclusion in that example was that it takes 0.00005 cubic centimeters or one-six hundred thousandth of an ounce of the back skin of this species to kill a mouse. In the back skin of one salamander there are an average 1380 poisonous granular glands and the way the arithmetic works out, only 0.069 or 69/1000 of *one* gland is sufficient to cause the death of the mouse. The back skin of the salamander is more toxic than the sides and belly, but the authorities agree that between 1200 and 2500 mice could be killed with the poison extracted from the skin of just one such salamander. The eggs of these salamanders are also known to contain high concentrations of poison.

It is possible that these toxins also function to keep the salamander free from infection since they may also inhibit parasites and bacteria.

The article goes on to say that one of the authors inadvertently jabbed a sharp tweezer point into his finger and within a few minutes there was an intense burning sensation followed by numbness which then progressed up the arm. The entire arm and shoulder were soon numb. This numbness persisted for a half hour and was accompanied by light-headedness. It is assumed that the tweezer had some salamander poison on it.

In still another case, a 26-year-old male in Oregon swallowed five *T. granulosa* on a dare and four hours later he was dizzy and his arms and legs tingled. By the fifth hour he was vomiting, and he continued for six hours when he was admitted to a hospital still nauseous and vomiting and dizzy. It took two days of treatment to get him back on his feet, recovered except that he was still dizzy when he turned his head. He was probably "dizzy" to begin with!

Evidence suggests that all the SALAMANDRIDAE are, to some extent, equipped with these poison glands. The precaution is simple.

1. Don't eat the skins and eggs of *T. granulosa*, or any other salamander.
2. Don't eat any uncooked CAUDATA. Better still, don't eat CAUDATA unless it was prepared by an experienced Japanese cook. Some Japanese cooks are specially licensed to cook pufferfish for this same reason.
3. Handle specimens with nets or gloves or cautiously.
4. Wash hands thoroughly after handling any tailed Amphibian.
5. Don't rub your eyes after handling amphibians. *It's only common sense!*

Diseases

Injuries to tail and toes are best left alone; it is likely that not only will there be healing but eventual regeneration of the lost digits and even sometimes limbs and tails. In fact, some salamander eyes, removed surgically, have been regenerated.

Skin infections are usually caused by foul water, overly warm water, crowding, toxins from other animals, and abrasion. Correct the source of trouble and bathe the specimen in any of the antibiotic solutions available in pet shops for aquarium fish. Use the dose recommended for fish and after a short treatment, generally one-half the time suggested for fish, return the specimen to his newly cleaned quarters. The biggest problems usually encountered come from crowding and uneaten food.

The most dread disease of captive amphibians is red leg. This is a bacterial infection caused by *Aeromonas hydrophilia* and the symptoms are reddening of the skin on the legs and other parts as well. The disease causes listlessness preceding death in about 50% of the cases. Epidemics are most liable to occur in September and October. It is probably the most contagious of diseases to which amphibia are subject.

Control of this disease is accomplished by removing any infected specimens, washing specimens and equipment in dilute potassium permanganate, cleanliness, circulation of fresh water, and finally, increase of salinity and acidity of water to the highest level that the specimens can tolerate—probably somewhat less than the salinity of their own body fluids, perhaps 0.5% or even 0.6% for short periods. A level tablespoon of granulated salt weighs about eleven grams and a gallon of water weighs 3785 grams; therfore, one tablespoon of salt in a gallon of water is 11/3785 or .0029 which also is 0.29%. Let's call it 0.3%. So then, a tablespoonful in a half gallon would be a 0.6% solution and you can take it from there. Incidentally, it would require about ten tablespoons of salt in a gallon of water to approximate the salinity of sea water.

Acidity to a pH of 3 is also desirable if your specimens can tolerate it. You can get an inexpensive pH kit at your pet shop.

Your veterinarian might suggest a drug to combat this bacterial infection, but *control* depends on the sanitary measures already mentioned.

If a specimen develops an unusual disease and dies from it, it may be advisable to investigate the cause. Animal pathology is highly specialized and not many people practice in this field. Your veterinarian may be interested or he may direct you to a specialist, but you should not expect your veterinarian to provide health services or an autopsy *gratis*. If the answer means something to you, you should be prepared to pay for the effort. If dead specimens are to be examined locally you might simply refrigerate the remains until they can be delivered. This leaves the tissues in the best condition for detailed examination short of a living organism. If mailing is involved, the specimen should be preserved in formalin.

Formaldehyde (37 to 40% solution) should be diluted with 9 or 10 volumes of water. Then it is called formalin. The body cavity should be opened to assure that the fixing process is more than skin deep. Of course a

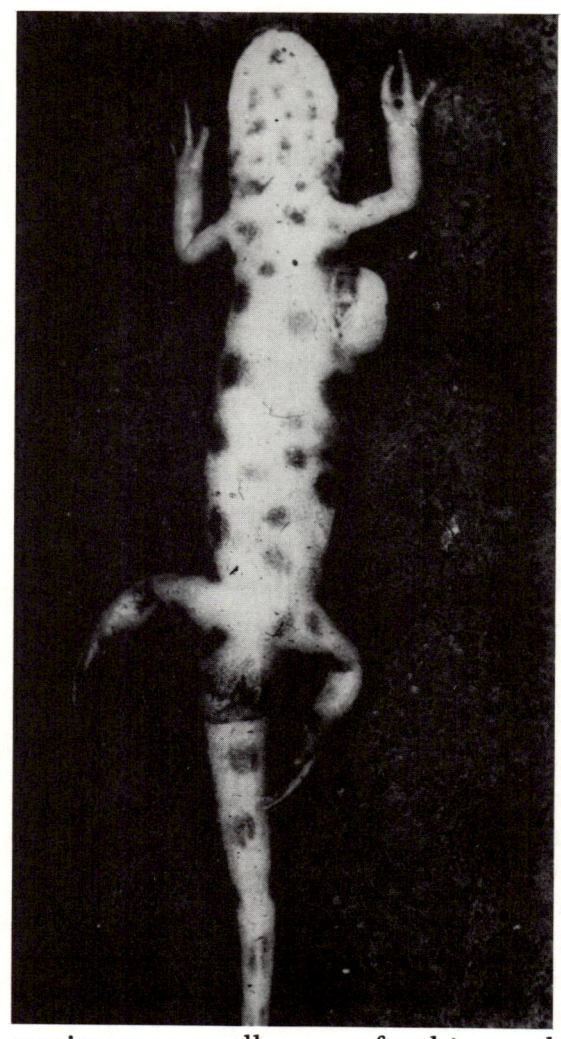

A smooth newt, *Triturus vulgaris*, caught in the wild with a ruptured body wall and a gastric hernia. Post mortem examination revealed that these conditions were caused by accumulated gas in the stomach resulting from fermented vegetable matter. Salamanders and newts are generally carnivorous animals. Offering the wrong kind of food can lead to harmful or fatal consequences. Photo by Dr. E. Elkan.

specimen as small as an eft, thinner than a pencil and but four inches long, need not be opened to be preserved.

Aquatic CAUDATA are susceptible to many of the same fungus, parasites and protozoan diseases as are fishes and if you have a specimen that suffers from an unknown ailment which resembles an ailment for which fish are treated, you might try the same fish treatment on the amphibian. Drugs and chemicals like copper sulphate, penicillin, quinine and Terramycin have been used to treat fish diseases. Many such preparations are available in pet shops or aquarium shops. Lacking specific knowledge of your animal's distress, treatment with a fish remedy—and in the same dosage—is the best last resort.

Before you start to dose your specimens, begin at the beginning. Most diseases of captive amphibians are brought on by crowded and unsanitary conditions and most of the remainder are caused by diet. Keep the aquarium clean and uncrowded. Remove and isolate sick or parasitized individuals. Pay strict attention to food and temperature requirements and be well on the way to the longevity records mentioned previously in this book.

The hookworm of the southern U.S. infests some salamanders as a parasite; so do tapeworms. Also, red mites sometimes attack captive salamanders. Most parasites go through cycles which require changing hosts or at least an intermediate host to reproduce themselves, and that is where you should catch them.

Isolate your captive CAUDATA from sources of infection and then work to eliminate the resident parasites. Hopefully your specimen will then remain parasite-free.

A cool supply of fresh water helps since it carries away spores, eggs and larvae of offending organisms. Brief washes in dilute potassium permanganate or copper sulphate are also effective in eliminating or reducing parasitic infestations.

One book, *Diseases of Amphibians*, by Drs. Elkan and Reichenbach-Kline, should be very helpful in the recognition and treatment of salamander disorders. It is published by T.F.H. Publications and is available through your pet shop.

Summing Up

Many of us open a book from the back, especially when we are browsing. For these readers, and also for more conventional readers who might enjoy a brief review: CAUDATA are relatively easy to maintain and some species will breed in captivity. The major points to keep in mind when caring for newts and other salamanders are listed here as a brief checklist.

Uneaten *food* should be removed before it decays. Waste products should be flushed or *filtered* out of the aquaria. Don't plan to cure *infections* but rather practice hygiene to avoid them.

Avoid crowding, *mixing of species*, and combining sizes unless you are certain the animals can tolerate each other.

Wash your hands after handling salamanders to avoid *toxins*.

Feed whole organisms and vary the *diet* to assure proper nutrition.

Keep salamanders cool. The *temperature* they need is nearly always less than that required by tropical fish, and it should be kept below 75° F. at all times.

Keep containers covered; many salamanders can crawl up vertical glass sides of *aquariums*.

Keep a culture of *live food* available for your pets to assure a constant supply.

Handle large specimens only when absolutely necessary and then use gloves or a net.

Join a *society* and share your experiences with others.

Avoid *endangered species*; there are plenty of interesting forms which are not endangered.

Demonstrate a humane interest in your pets or give them to a zoo or *herpetologist* who will.

SELECTED READING LIST

Bishop, S.C. 1941. *The Salamanders of New York.* New York State Museum Bulletin No. 324.

―――――. 1943. *Handbook of Salamanders of U.S. and Canada.* Comstock, Ithaca, New York.

Breen, J.F. 1974. *Encyclopedia of Reptiles and Amphibians.* TFH Publications, Neptune City, New Jersey.

Cochran, Doris. 1961. *Living Amphibians of the World.* Doubleday, New York.

Conant, R. 1975. *Field Guide to Reptiles and Amphibians of Eastern North America.* Houghton-Mifflin, Boston.

Dowling, H.G. (ed.) 1974. *Yearbook of Herpetology.* Dept. of Biology, New York University, New York City, New York.

Noble, G.K. 1931. *The Biology of the Amphibia.* McGraw Hill, New York. Also 1954 reprint by Dover, New York.

Porter, K.R. 1972. *Herpetology.* Saunders, Philadelphia, Pennsylvania.

Stebbins, R.C. 1966. *Field Guide to Western Reptiles and Amphibians.* Houghton-Mifflin, Boston.

Index

Page numbers printed in *italic* type refer to photographs.

Aeromonas hydrophilia, 90
Ambystoma, 43, 73, *76*, *79*, *82*
  annulatum, 30, *33*
  jeffersonianum, *31*, 32
  macrodactylum, *36*
  maculatum, *6*, 31, *37*, *66*
  mexicanum, *32*, 81, 83
  opacum, *31*, 33
  talpoideum, 31
  texanum, 31
  tigrinum, *28*, 31, 32, 83
  tigrinum velasci, 29
Ambystomatoidea, 11, 14, 30, 58
Amphibia, 10, 11, 15, 80, 88
Amphiuma, 27, 42
  means, 27, *30*, 51
  pholeter, 27
  tridactylum, 27
Amphiumidae, 14, 27
Andrias, 46
  maximus, 51
Aneides
  aeneus, 47
  ferreus, *52*
  lugubris, 46, 47, *53*
Animalia, 11
Anurans, 10
Artemia salina, 80
Axolotl, 31

Breeding in captivity, 78-85
Brine shrimp, *60*

Caecilians, 10
Caudata, 10, 11, 14, 19, 42, 46, 47, 50
Chironomus, 80
Chordata, 11
Congo eels, 14
Craneflies, *53*
Crayfish, *4*
Crested newt, 12
Cryptobranchidae, 14, 18
Cryptobranchoidea, 11, 14
Cryptobranchus, 4
  alleganiensis, *5*, 18
Cynops, 23

Daphnia, 23, 38, 80, 83
Desmognathus, 34, 35, 50
  fuscus, *40*
  fuscus fuscus, 86
  ochrophaeus, 85
  wrighti, 50

Dicamptodon, 46
Diseases, 90
Diseases of Amphibians, 93
Drosophila, 72

Earthworms, *60*, *71*
Euproctus, 38
Eurycea
  bislineata, *59*, 86
  longicauda, *41*
  lucifuga, *34*, *41*, *65*
  multiplicata, 58

Foods, 70-72
Frog eggs, 24

Gymnophiona, 10
Gyrinophilus porphyriticus, 86

Haideotriton wallacei, *62*
Hemidactylium, 39
  scutatum, 47
Housing, 67
Hydromantes, 56
  genei, *35*
Hynobiidae, 14, 18

Leurognathus, 34
Lissamphibia, 11
Live Foods for Aquarium and Terrarium Animals, 70
Lungless salamanders, 14

Mealworms, 72
Megalobatrachus, 46
Mole salamanders, 14
Mountain brook newts, 38
Mudpuppies, 14, 26

Necturus maculosus, 26
Newts, 10, 11, 14, 43
Notophthalmus, 23
  viridescens, *20*, 23, *64*, 81
  viridescens dorsalis, *74*
  viridescens viridescens, *21*, 86

Olms, 14
Onychodactylus japonicus, 47

Paramesotriton, 23
Plethodon, 35, 39, 43, 47, 53
  cinereus, *44*, *45*, *87*
  glutinosus, *48*
  richmondi, *48*

Plethodontidae, 14, 34, 59, 62, 6
Pleurodeles waltl, *50*, 81
Population density, 86
Proteidae, 14, 23
Proteoidea, 11
Proteus, 26
  anguinus, *26*
Pseudobranchus, 19, 22
Pseudoeurycea, 56
  belli, 57
  cephalica, 56
  species, 57
Pseudotriton ruber, *40*

Red eft, *24*
Regeneration, 66
Reproduction, 76
Respiration, 73
Ribbed newt, 49, *50*

Salamandra salamandra, 42, 46, 51, 81
Salamandroidea, 11, 14, 22, 59, 88
Salentia, 10
Siren, *4*, 22, 19
  atra, 47
  intermedia, *5*, 22
  lacertina, 22
Sirenoidea, 11, 14, 19

Taricha, 23
  granulosa, *25*
The American Natural History, 19
The Larousse Encyclopedia of Animal Life, 22
Toxins, 88
Triturus
  alpestris, *8*, *16*, *77*, 81
  cristatus, *12*, *13*, 81
  granulosa, 89
  helveticus, *17*, 81
  marmoratus, 27
  pyrrhogaster, 51
  vulgaris, 81, *92*
Tubifex worms, 23, 72, 80
Typhlotriton spelaeus, *63*

Urodela, 14

Waterdogs, 14, 26